W9-CLY-994

The Faithful Friend

THE FAITHFUL FRIEND

Favorite Writings About

Owning and Loving Dogs

Selected by Lois Daniel

with Color Photographs

and Historical Illustrations

Hallmark Editions

Acknowledgments

»Traveling With Charley« from *Travels With Charley* by John Steinbeck. Copyright © 1961, 1962 by The Curtis Publishing Co., Inc., copyright © 1962 by John Steinbeck. Reprinted by permission of The Viking Press, Inc. and McIntosh and Otis, Inc. »The Prayer of the Dog« from *Prayers From the Ark* by Carmen Bernos de Gasztold, translated by Rumer Godden. Copyright © 1962 by Rumer Godden. Reprinted by permission of The Viking Press, Inc. and Curtis Brown Ltd. Selections from *King Solomon's Ring* by Konrad Z. Lorenz, translated by Mrs. M. Latzke. Copyright 1952 by Thomas Y. Crowell Company, New York, publishers, and reprinted in the U.S. with their permission. Reprinted elsewhere with permission from Methuen & Company, Ltd. Selections from *Dogs Against the Darkness* by Dickson Hartwell reprinted by permission of Dodd, Mead & Company, Inc. Copyright © 1942, 1960, 1968 by Dickson Hartwell. »The Foundling« reprinted by permission of Dodd, Mead & Company, Inc. from *The Rin Tin Tin Story* by James W. English. Copyright 1949 by James W. English. »A Friendly Bloodhound« by Lowell Thomas from *The Pageant of Life*. Reprinted by permission of the author. »Owney, The Post Office Dog« from *Dogs of Destiny* by Fairfax Downey. Copyright 1949 by Fairfax Downey. Reprinted by permission of the publishers, Charles Scribner's Sons. »Little Lost Pup« from *Death And General Putnam and* 101 *Other Poems* by Arthur Guiterman. Copyright, 1935, by E. P. Dutton & Co., Inc. Renewal, ©, 1963 by Mrs. Vida Lindo Guiterman. Reprinted by permission of the publishers. »The Ambiguous Dog« from *The Laughing Muse* by Arthur Guiterman. Reprinted by permission of Mrs. Arthur Guiterman. Selection from *Dogs at War* by Clayton G. Going. Copyright 1944 by Clayton G. Going. Reprinted by permission of The Macmillan Company, publisher. »All the Good Dogs« from *Dogs and People* by George and Helen Papashvily. Copyright 1954 by George and Helen Papashvily. Reprinted by arrangement with the publishers, J. B. Lippincott. »Dog Diplomacy« from *Dogs and People* by George and Helen Papashvily. Copyright 1954 by George and Helen Papashvily. Reprinted by arrangement with the publishers, J. B. Lippincott. »Dog Asleep« by Margaret Mackprang Mackay. Reprinted by permission of G. P. Putnam's Sons. »The Road to Vagabondia« from *Poems* by Dana Burnet. Copyright 1935 by Harper & Brothers; renewed 1943 by Dana Burnet. Reprinted by permission of Harper & Row, publishers. »What Companion Like a Dog?« by John Burroughs from *The Heart of John Burroughs Journal*. Reprinted by permission of the publisher, Houghton Mifflin Company.

Printed in the United States of America.
Library of Congress Catalog Card Number: 68:8818.

The Gentle Pet

The First Friend

When the Man waked up he said,
»What is Wild Dog doing here?«
And the Woman said,
»His name is not Wild Dog any more,
but the First Friend,
because he will be our friend
for always and always and always.«

Rudyard Kipling

Good Company

Let us not lie to ourselves that we need the dog as a protection for our house. We *do* need him, but not as a watch-dog. I, at least in dreary foreign towns, have certainly stood in need of my dog's company and I have derived, from the mere fact of his existence, a great sense of inward security, such as one finds in a childhood memory or in the prospect of the scenery of one's own home country, for me the Blue Danube, for you, perhaps, the White Cliffs of Dover. In the almost film-like flitting-by of modern life, a man needs something to tell him, from time to time, that he is still himself, and nothing can give him this assurance in so comforting a manner as the »four feet trotting behind.«

Konrad Lorenz

»What Companion Like a Dog?«

So great is my need of a comrade, an untalking companion, on my walks, or boating, or about the farm; and, next to one's bosom friend, what companion like a dog? Your thought is his thought, your wish is his wish, and where you desire to go, that place of all others is preferable to him. It was bliss enough for Rab to be with me, and it was a never-failing source of pleasure for me to be with Rab. . . .

My dog is interested in everything I do. Then he represents the spirit of holiday, of fun, of adventure. The world is full of wonders to him, and in a journey of a mile he has many adventures. Every journey is an excursion, a sally into an unknown land, teeming with curiosities. A dog lives only ten or fifteen years, but think how much he crowds into that space, how much energy and vitality he lives up!

John Burroughs

The Gentle Pet

The dog hath so himself subdued
That hunger cannot make him rude;
And his behavior doth confess
True courage dwells in gentleness.
Few men to do such noble deeds have learned,
Or having done, could look so unconcerned.

Anonymous

If We Had To Serve

It is a long work to organize a happy existence upon the borderland of two such different worlds as the world of beasts and the world of men. How should we fare if we had to serve—while remaining within our own sphere—a divinity, not an imaginary one, like ourselves, because the offspring of our own brain, but a god actually visible, ever present, ever active and as foreign, as superior to our being as we are to the dog?

Maurice Maeterlinck

A cherished companion, the dog has embellished the crests of aristocracy, as in this 18th century heraldic design from the Szoeke File.

Eulogy on the Dog

(Delivered at the trial of a man who had shot his neighbor's dog)

Gentlemen of the Jury: The best friend a man has in this world may turn against him and become his enemy. His son or his daughter, that he has reared with loving care, may prove ungrateful. Those who are nearest and dearest to us, those whom we trust with our happiness and our good name, may become traitors to their faith. The money that a man has he may lose. It flies away from him, perhaps when he needs it most. A man's reputation may be sacrificed in a moment of ill-considered action. The people who are prone to fall on their knees to do us honor when success is with us may be the first to throw stones of malice when failure settles its cloud upon our heads. The one absolutely unselfish friend that man can have in this selfish world, the one that never deserts him, the one that never proves ungrateful or treacherous, is his dog. Gentlemen of the Jury: A man's dog stands by him in prosperity and in poverty, in health and in sickness. He will sleep on the cold ground, where the wintry winds blow and the snow drives fiercely, if only he may be near his master's side. He will kiss the hand that has no food to offer, he will lick the wounds and sores that come in encounter with the roughness of the world. He guards the sleep of his pauper master as if he were a prince. When all other friends desert, he remains. When riches take wings and reputation falls to pieces, he is as constant in his love as the sun in its journey through the heavens. If fortune drives the master forth an outcast in the world, friendless, and homeless, the faithful dog asks no higher privilege than that of accompanying him to guard against danger, to fight against his enemies. And, when the last scene of all comes, and death takes the master in its embrace, and his body is laid away in the cold ground, no matter if all other friends pursue their way, there by his graveside will the noble dog be found, his head between his paws, his eyes sad but open in alert watchfulness, faithful and true even to death.

Senator George G. Vest

A Superior Companion

Dogs are much superior to human beings as companions. They do not quarrel or argue with you. They never talk about themselves but listen to you while you talk about yourself, and keep up an appearance of being interested in the conversation. They never make stupid remarks.

They never say unkind things. They never tell us our faults, »merely for our own good.« They do not at inconvenient moments mildly remind us of our past follies and mistakes. They never inform us, as our inamoratas sometimes do, that we are not nearly so nice as we used to be. We are always the same to them. He is very imprudent, a dog is. He never makes it his business to inquire whether you are in the right or in the wrong, never bothers as to whether you are going up or down upon life's ladder, never asks whether you are rich or poor, silly or wise, sinner or saint. You are his pal. That is enough for him, and come luck or misfortune, good repute or bad, honor or shame, he is going to stick to you, to comfort you, guard you, give his life for you, if need be —foolish, brainless, soulless dog!

Jerome K. Jerome

»He Is At Our Side«

As our human annals stretch, he is at our side, as at present; but what are human annals in comparison with the times of which we have no witness? The fact remains that he is there in our houses, as ancient, as rightly placed, as perfectly adapted to our habits as though he had appeared on this earth, such as he now is, at the same time as ourselves.

We have not to gain his confidence or his friendship: he is born our friend; while his eyes are still closed, already he believes in us: even before his birth, he has given himself to man.

But the word »friend« does not exactly depict his affectionate worship. He loves us and reveres us as though we had drawn him out of nothing. He is, before all, our creature full of gratitude and more devoted than the apple of our eye. He is our intimate and impassioned slave, whom nothing discourages, whom nothing repels, whose ardent trust and love nothing can impair.

He has solved, in an admirable and touching manner, the terrifying problem which human wisdom would have to solve if a divine race came to occupy our globe. He has loyally, religiously, irrevocably recognized man's superiority and has surrendered himself to him body and soul, without afterthought, without any intention to go back, reserving of his independence, his instinct and his character only the small part indispensable to the continuation of the life prescribed by nature.

With an unquestioning certainty, an unconstraint and a simplicity that surprise us a little, deeming us better and more powerful than all that exists, he betrays, for our benefit, the whole of the animal kingdom to which he belongs and, without scruple, denies his race, his kin, his mother and his young.

Maurice Maeterlinck

At Peace

If a man does not soon pass beyond the thought:»By what shall this dog profit me?« into the large state of simple gladness to be with the dog, he shall never know the very essence of that companionship which depends, not on the points of a dog, but on some strange and subtle mingling of mute spirits. For it is by muteness that a dog becomes for one so utterly beyond value; with him one is at peace, where words play no torturing tricks. When he just sits loving and knows that he is being loved, those are the moments that I think are precious to a dog;—when, with his adoring soul coming through his eyes, he feels that you are really thinking of him.

John Galsworthy

Dog and Man

Hours have passed. You have sat bent over your work. Following your searching, winging thoughts, your glance turns up and aside. There your eyes meet two other eyes, which, who shall say how long already or why, have been watching you from the depths of the chair in which your friend is curled up. No sound, no movement, nothing but two pair of eyes which in the buzzing silence of the room meet, and in that meeting become aware of unexpected happiness. He wags his tail, scarcely perceptibly, but

immovably he keeps looking at you, with persistent gentleness, as if he feared that by and by immeasurable seas will separate him from you again.

But these wide seas. They separate you even now, gulfs of spiritual and bodily differences not to be bridged. You are indeed out of each other's reach and yet, at the same time, touchingly near. You ask for miracles; here is one of the miracles surrounding you which you so carelessly pass by. For is not this wonder greater than the meeting of two souls who can measure each other's virtues and needs in the depths of their own hearts?

This is the meeting of two souls flying to each other from two worlds which are irrevocably separated, different in kind, in aim, and destination. And yet, just as a power that moves the universe rushes through the infinite, incalculable distances, so a small spark of that same power can do away with all distances and separations between two beings and kindle the desire for warmth in their hearts.

Roland Holst

A Tribute

The dog, independently of his beauty, voracity, strength and swiftness, has all the interior qualities which can attract the regard of man. The tame dog comes to lay at his master's feet his courage, strength and talents, and waits his orders to use them; he consults, interrogates and beseeches; the glance of his eye is sufficient, he understands the signs of his will.

Without the vices of man he has all the ardor of sentiment; and, what is more, he has fidelity and consistency in his affections; no ambition, no interest, no desire of revenge, no fear but that of displeasing him; he is all zeal, all warmth, and all obedience.

Georges-Louis Leclerc Buffon

Choose a Dog

If you want a personal contact, if you are a lonely person and want, like Byron, »to know there is an eye will mark your coming and look brighter when you come,« then choose a dog. Do not think it is cruel to keep a dog in a town flat. His happiness depends largely upon how much time you can spend with him and upon how often he may accompany you on an errand. He does not mind waiting for hours at your study door if he is finally rewarded by a ten minutes' walk at your side. Personal friendship means everything to a dog; but remember, it entails no small responsibility, for a dog is not a servant to whom you can easily give notice. And remember, too, if you are an over-sensitive person, that the life of your friend is much shorter than your own and a sad parting after ten or fifteen years is inevitable.

Konrad Lorenz

All His Good and Gain

Command; he thee obeys most readily.
Strike him; he whines and falls down at thy feet.
Call him: he leaves his game and comes to thee
With wagging tail, offering his service meek.

If so thou wilt, a collar he will wear;
And when thou wish to take it off again,
Unto thy feet he crouchest down most fair,
As if thy will were all his good and gain.

J. Molle

Dog Diplomacy

Dogs are infinitely courteous. Offer one water and, thirsty or not, he takes several laps to repay you for the trouble. He comes after meals to express his thanks for them. Step accidentally on a tail or paw and after the first yelp of surprise he offers you repeated reassurances: *I'm* not a *bit* hurt, and *you* aren't at *all* clumsy.

Dogs have, not a slave's, but rather a diplomat's quickness in guessing a mood. They respond with tact and sympathy and understanding. They imply no criticism, pass no judgment, offer no useless or self-concerned advice—all highly desirable qualities in a friend.

Great men always have dogs, said Ouida, the English novelist, because, »they find the world so full of parasites, toadies, liars, fawners, hypocrites; the incorruptible candor, loyalty and honor of the dog are like so much water in a barren place to the thirsty traveller.«

George and Helen Papashvily

A Dog's Worship

Man is the god of the dog; he knows no other; he can understand no other. And see how he worships him! with what dependence he looks up to him! with what cheerful alacrity he obeys him! His whole soul is wrapt up in his god! all the powers and faculties of his nature are devoted to his service! and these powers and faculties are ennobled by the intercourse....

Divines tell us that it just ought to be so with Christians—but the dog puts the Christian to shame.

Robert Burns

Dog Asleep

You sprawl upon your special bed
In peaceful somnolence; your head
At rest, with gently breathing snout,
And one ear lying wrong side out.

All's quiet,
Then a little quirk
Disturbs your upper lip. You jerk
Your paws with tiny rhythmic quivers,
Your tail is stiff, your stomach shivers.
Your furry body spread supine
Begins to tremble and a whine
Disturbs your sleep. You try to run
With all your might, to dodge the one
Who seems to chase you; and you yelp
Aloud, as if in need of help.

Caressing you, I say, »Wake up!
It's just a dream you foolish pup!«
You blink and startle willy-nilly,
And promptly feel extremely silly.

Margaret Mackay

The Favorite and the Famous

»My Boxer, Lance«

Dog owners in the United States loaned their pets to the U.S. Army during World War II. In the following letter written to Dogs for Defense, the organization which became the famous K-9 Corps, a young boy expresses his concern:

My Boxer, Lance, was in the Army since last June. I have not heard anything about him since I received a certificate from the Quartermaster General. The number on it was 11281.

I love Lance very much and want to know if he is doing anything brave.

Can you please tell me where he is and what kind of a job he does? Please answer soon because I can't wait much longer to know what has become of him.

The Dog Who Circled the World

Clerks of the Albany, New York, post office, found a little mongrel curled up on a mail sack one morning in 1888. A wistful wag of his tail won him a share of their lunch. They could not bear turning the thin, shivering creature out into the cold. Adopted and named Owney, the dog stayed until the day when the sack he used as a bed was picked up and filled with letters. He followed it into a mail car. Owney was off on his celebrated travels.

Though he was soon sent back to Albany, his post office friends bought him a collar, marked with his name and address, in case he strayed again. It was a wise precaution. Owney, gripped by the travel urge, soon began boarding trains at every opportunity. Mail-car clerks enjoyed his company. Cared for like a registered letter, Owney »mailed« himself to most of the cities and large towns of the United States, with excursions into Canada and Mexico, and his pals of the postal service »postmarked« him by attaching tags to his collar. Trip after trip hung so much weight on the dog's neck that the Postmaster General presented him with a special harness to carry tags and conferred on him a frank entitling him to ride free with the U.S. mail. The city of San Francisco added a traveling bag, fitted with a comb and brush, and a dog-blanket.

Owney, returning from a jaunt to Alaska in 1895, was visiting Tacoma, Washington, when he was observed eyeing mail sacks being loaded aboard the *S.S. Victoria* with a calculating look which seemed to say, »Mails go abroad. Why shouldn't I?« Friends hastily provided him with a letter of introduction to postal people everywhere, and he trotted up the gangplank. Making the voyage as the captain's guest, Owney landed in Japan, where he was received and decorated by the Mikado. The Emperor of China similarly honored him, as did personages all along his homeward route via the Suez Canal and at European ports. More than 200 medals and scrolls crammed Owney's baggage when his ship docked in New York. There the globe-trotter without delay caught an express for the West and reached Tacoma, his starting point, to establish a canine record of circling the world in 132 days.

Fairfax Downey

On A Favorite Lap Dog

I never barked when out of season;
I never bit without a reason;
I ne'er insulted weaker brother;
Nor wrong'd by force nor fraud another;
Though brutes are plac'd a rank below,
Happy for man could he say so!

Thomas Blacklock

The Road to Vagabondia

He was sitting on the doorstep
as I went strolling by;
A lonely little beggar
with a wistful, homesick eye—
And he wasn't what you'd borrow,
and he wasn't what you'd steal,
But I guessed his heart was breaking,
so I whistled him to heel.

They had stoned him through the city streets,
and naught the city cared,
But I was heading outward,
and the roads are sweeter shared,
So I took him for a comrade,
and I whistled him away—
On the road to Vagabondia,
that lies across the day!

Yellow dog he was; but bless you—
he was just the chap for me!
For I'd rather have an inch of dog
than miles of pedigree.
So we stole away together,
on the road that has no end,
With a new-coined day to fling away
and all the stars to spend!

Oh, to walk the road at morning,
when the wind is blowing clean,
And the yellow daisies fling their gold
across a world of green—
For the wind it heals the heartache,
and the sun it dries the scars,
On the road to Vagabondia
that lies beneath the stars.

'Twas the wonder of our going
cast a spell about our feet—
And we walked because the world was young,
because the way was sweet;
And we slept in wild-rose meadows
by the little wayside farms,
Till the Dawn came up the highroad
with the dead moon in her arms.

Oh, the Dawn it went before us
through a shining lane of skies,
And the Dream was at our heartstrings,
and the Light was in our eyes,
And we made no boast of glory
and we made no boast of birth,
On the road to Vagabondia
that lies across the earth!

Dana Burnet

Epitaph To A Dog

Near this spot
Are deposited the Remains
of one
Who possessed Beauty
Without Vanity,
Strength without Insolence,
Courage without Ferocity,
And all the Virtues of Man
Without his Vices.
This Praise, which would be unmeaning flattery
If inscribed over Human Ashes,
Is but a just tribute to the Memory of
»Boatswain,« a Dog
Who was born in Newfoundland,
May, 1803,
And died at Newstead Abbey
Nov. 18, 1808.

George Gordon, Lord Byron

Frenchie

I found him in a shell-hole,
With a gash across his head,
Standing guard beside his master,
Though he knew the boy was dead.

Hell was raining all around us,
We could only lie there tight,
Got to sort o' like each other
Through the misery of that night.

When I crawled back to the trenches,
—And I took his master, too—
Frenchie followed. Guess he figured,
Just because of that, I'd do.

You wouldn't say he's handsome,
He's been hit a dozen times—
But when we boys »go over,«
Over *with* us Frenchie climbs. . . .

And when for home I'm starting,
If I live to see this through,
Just one thing is sure as shooting;
That my dog is going, too.

Sgt. Frank C. McCarthy

Six Feet

My little rough dog and I
Live a life that is rather rare.
We have so many good walks to take
And so few hard things to bear;
So much that gladdens and re-creates,
So little of wear and tear.

Sometimes it blows and rains,
But still the six feet ply:
No care at all to the following four
If the leading two know why.
'Tis a pleasure to have six feet, we think,
My little rough dog and I.

And we travel all one way;
'Tis a thing we should never do,
To reckon the two without the four
Or the four without the two.
It would not be right if anyone tried,
Because it would not be true.

And who shall look up and say
That it ought not so to be,
Tho' the earth is Heaven enough for him,
Is it less than that to me?
For a little rough dog can make a joy
That enters eternity! *Author Unknown*

A Little Lost Pup

He was lost!—Not a shade of doubt of that;
For he never barked at a slinking cat,
But stood in the square where the wind blew raw,
With a drooping ear, and a trembling paw,
And a mournful look in his pleading eye,
And a plaintive sniff at the passer-by
That begged as plain as a tongue could sue,
»Oh, Mister, please may I follow you?«
A lorn, wee waif of a tawny brown
Adrift in the roar of a heedless town.
Oh, the saddest of sights in a world of sin
Is a little lost pup with his tail tucked in!

Well, he won my heart (for I set great store
On my own red Bute, who is here no more)
So I whistled clear, and he trotted up,
And who so glad as that small lost pup?

Now he shares my board, and he owns my bed,
And he fairly shouts when he hears my tread.
Then if things go wrong, as they sometimes do,
And the world is cold, and I'm feeling blue,
He asserts his right to assuage my woes
With a warm, red tongue and a nice, cold nose,
And a silky head on my arm or knee,
And a paw as soft as a paw can be.

When we rove the woods for a league about
He's as full of pranks as a school let out;
For he romps and frisks like a three-months colt,
And he runs me down like a thunder-bolt.
Oh, the blithest of sights in the world so fair
Is a gay little pup with his tail in air!

Arthur Guiterman

Cluny

I am quite sure he thinks that I am God—
Since He is God on whom each one depends
For life, and all things that His bounty sends—
My dear old dog, most constant of all friends;
Not quick to mind, but quicker far than I
To Him whom God I know and own; his eye
Deep brown and liquid, watches for my nod;
He is more patient underneath the rod
Than I, when God His wise corrections sends.
He looks love at me, deep as words e'er spake;
And from me never crumb or sup will take
But he wags thanks with his most vocal tail,
And when some crashing noise wakes all his fear
He is content and quiet if I'm near,
Secure that my protection will prevail;
So, faithful, mindful, thankful, trustful, he
Tells me what I unto my God should be.

Bishop George Washington Doan

The dog, a natural hunter, has aided man in his search

since the beginning of civilization.

Epitaph

His friends he loved. His direst earthly foes—
Cats—I believe he did but feign to hate.
My hand will miss the insinuated nose,
Mine eyes the tail that wagg'd contempt at fate.

Sir William Watson

Your Dog

I ask you, Master, just as dog to man,
(Explain it in our language, if you can)
Why Tabby, there, should have nine lives to live,
When I, *your dog,* have only one to give?

A cat! She's always greedy for her cream,
And cares for nothing but to doze and dream;
So smug and satisfied, she maddens me!
(She knows I hate her, sitting on *your* knee.)

You taught me, Master, everything I know.
Your friend is my friend—and your foe, my foe.
Can Tabby tell, or does she think she can,
How close a one-man dog lives to *his man*?

Once, when you lost your bearings in the fog,
Who was so keen to find you as your dog?
Did Tabby feel your danger, scent your track,
And leave her cozy hearth to bring you back?

When we came limping home, what did she do?
Just waked up long enough to yawn, »That you?«
Oh, yes, a cat may have nine lives to live,
But tell me, has she even one to give?

That stormy night you found me, picked me up—
A friendless, starving, vagrant little pup—
And brought me home, and named me, it was sweet
To lay my one life wholly at your feet!

It isn't that I'm jealous of the cat.
She may have nine, or ninety lives, at that.
But just to see her sitting on *your* knee,
Gosh, Master, lem'me run her up that tree!

Elizabeth P. Morse

The Foundling

An American sergeant, with a warm spot in his heart for dogs, befriended a helpless young puppy on the battlefields of France during the First World War and in so doing changed the course of his own life. However, at the time the soldier found the scrawny, newborn son of a German war dog, he was just an American boy a long way from home, and he was lonesome.

Back in California he had always had dogs of his own, had enjoyed their companionship, and the prospect of this puppy dying of cold and hunger was too much for a person who loved animals. The soldier placed the tiny ball of damp fur in the pocket of his jacket and came back to camp.

That day has remained in the sergeant's mind with indelible clarity, for the forlorn, half-starved puppy became the greatest animal star in the history of motion pictures and for a decade earned over one hundred thousand dollars annually for his master and friend, Lee Duncan. The pup grew up to be the famous movie star, Rin Tin Tin.

James W. English

Flush or Faunus

You see this dog; it was but yesterday
I mused forgetful of his presence here
Till thought on thought drew downward tear on tear;
When from the pillow where wet-cheeked I lay,
A head as hairy as Faunus thrust its way
Right sudden against my face, two golden-clear
Great eyes astonished mine, a drooping ear
Did flap me on either cheek to dry the spray!
I started first as some Arcadian
Amazed by goatly god in twilight grove:
But as the bearded vision closelier ran
My tears off, I knew Flush, and rose above
Surprise and sadness—thanking the true Pan
Who by low creatures leads to heights of love.

Elizabeth Barrett Browning

An Old Dog Dies

The following editorial appeared in the New York Herald Tribune *on the occasion of the death of President Franklin D. Roosevelt's dog Fala:*

He probably was the most famous dog of his time, a fact which surely cheered his old age a little bit. Like all dogs, he was essentially nonpolitical, though it cannot be denied that his name was prominently mentioned in at least one notable political speech. But unlike most dogs, he kept getting his name and picture in the papers. Not even Rin Tin Tin was better known, and Rin Tin Tin had to work to gain friends and fans. Not he. He just sat back and waited, and let them come to him.

And come they did, in such profusion that it was all an honest dog could do to keep them straight. Presidents, Prime Ministers, Kings and such—pleasant people they were, too, never too busy for a pat on the head or a kindly word. That jolly man with the cigar on the battleship, drawing up some kind of document—he was a person any dog would be proud to have as a friend. And that pleasant garden party in the back of the house, with the kind foreign lady and gentleman—you could tell that was a royal occasion because they served frankfurters, food fit for a king. And the Boss himself—well, after all, any good dog is a one-man dog at heart.

It was too bad that they had to go away, these people, but that seems to be the way of the human world. And after awhile there is nothing to do, really, except follow them. Certainly it's far better to slip gently away than to drag out your days amid your faded memories and packs of impertinent pups who hardly even know your name is Fala.

My Dog

I have no dog, but it must be
Somewhere there's one belongs to me—
A little chap with wagging tail,
And dark brown eyes that never quail,
But look you through, and through, and through,
With love unspeakable and true.

Somewhere it must be, I opine,
There is a little dog of mine
With cold black nose that sniffs around
In search of what things may be found
In pocket or some nook hard by
Where I have hid them from his eye.

Somewhere my doggie pulls and tugs
The fringes of rebellious rugs,
Or with the mischief of the pup
Chews all my shoes and slippers up,
And when he's done it to the core,
With eyes all eager, pleads for more.

Somewhere upon his hinder legs
My little doggie sits and begs,
And in a wistful minor tone
Pleads for the pleasures of the bone—
I pray it be his owner's whim
To yield, and grant the same to him.

Somewhere a little dog doth wait;
It may be by some garden gate.
With eyes alert and tail attent—
You know the kind of tail that's meant—
With stores of yelps of glad delight
To bid me welcome home at night.

Somewhere a little dog is seen,
His nose two shaggy paws between,
Flat on his stomach, one eye shut
Held fast in dreamy slumber, but
The other open, ready for
His master coming through the door.

John Kendrick Bangs

To A Little Deaf Dog

What do you think, dear little friend,
Of the silence that has come?
Why do you think—poor little friend—
The voices loved are dumb?

Does the simple creed of perfect love,
That held you firm all through,
Still fill your faithful little life
And make it right for you?

From your deep eyes the same old trust
Beams up into my own,
And from the joy that in them lies—
You do not feel alone.

But when with head upon my knee
You gaze so wistfully,
I hope, old man, you understand
The fault lies not in me.

I trust that you who know so much,
And yet so little too,
Through your sweet dog philosophy
Know that my love holds true.

Ethellyn Brewer DeFoe

The Prayer of the Dog

Lord,
I keep watch!
If I am not here
who will guard their house?
Watch over their sheep?
Be faithful?
No one but You and I
understands
what faithfulness is.
They call me, »Good dog! Nice dog!«
Words . . .
I take their pats
and the old bones they throw me
and I seem pleased.
They really believe they make me happy.
I take kicks too
when they come my way.
None of that matters.
I keep watch!
Lord,
do not let me die
until, for them,
all danger is driven away.
Amen.

Carmen Bernos De Gastold

All the Good Dogs

A Loyal Guide

In the devastating New England hurricane of 1938, a blind master and his dog were on the streets at the height of the storm. It was almost impossible to stand up against the wind. Trees were crashing down and bringing with them telephones and live high tension lines. As the dog guided its master along the debris-strewn sidewalk, the man put himself completely in the animal's care. He knew he was not being guided in a straight line but was zigzagging back and forth in order to avoid fallen branches.

In the middle of one block, however, the dog stopped. After a moment or two it made a few hesitant steps first to the right and then to the left. Finally it went across the street in the middle of the block opposite the sidewalk, traversed the front yard of a residence—the blind man could feel a soft, rain-soaked lawn under his feet—went around to the back of a house and emerged through a driveway two houses beyond, recrossed the sidewalk and street again to the side where they had previously been walking and continued warily on to their destination.

The next day the blind man remarked to a friend that there must have been a large tree down in the middle of that block, otherwise his dog would not have made such a detour. But his friend said, no, there hadn't been any tree down, only some high tension wires were strewn along the street at that point. If the dog had let him touch one of them, the result would have been electrocution. . . .

Dickson Hartwell

A Friendly Bloodhound

Ever since the days of Uncle Tom and his cabin, we've been taught to look upon the bloodhound as a ferocious beast. Even his name sounds fierce. However, consider the following:

In Oklahoma some officers of the law were looking for a couple of public enemies, a man and a woman who had committed several robberies. The bloodhounds were put on the traces of the two, but nothing happened. Several days later a man and a woman strolled into a restaurant. They were followed by an unusual looking but exceedingly amiable and gentle dog. The animal hunched down and watched them while they ordered breakfast.

Just as they were beginning to eat their scrambled eggs, in walked the sergeant of the Missouri highway patrol. He promptly arrested the man and woman. They were the couple so badly wanted by the law. The dog was one of the bloodhounds that had been set on their trail.

The man told the policeman: »Why, we thought that was just some farmer's coon dog. He was so friendly, we took him along.«

Lowell Thomas

A Drinking Dog

Here is an old story I remember of a Newfoundland dog—an immense black, good-humored Newfoundland dog. He came from Oxford and had lived all his life at a brewery. Instructions were given with him that if he were let out every morning alone, he would immediately find out the river, regularly take a swim, and gravely come home again.

This he did with great punctuality, but after a little while was observed to smell of beer. The lady was so sure that he smelt of beer that she resolved to watch him.

Accordingly, he was seen to come back from his swim round the usual corner, and go up a flight of steps into a beer-shop. Being instantly followed, the shopkeeper is seen to take down a pewter pot, and is heard to say: »Well, old chap, come for your beer as usual, have you?« Upon which he draws a pint and puts it down and the dog drinks it.

Being required to explain how this comes to pass, the man says, »Yes, ma'am, I know he's your dog, ma'am, but I didn't when he first come. He looked in, ma'am—as a brickmaker might—and then he come in—as a brickmaker might—and he wagged his tail at the pots, and he give a sniff round and conveyed to me as he was used to beer. So I drawed him a drop, and he drunk it up. Next morning he come agen by the clock and I drawed him a pint, and ever since he has took 'is pint reg'lar.«

Charles Dickens

Guarding His Master

Suddenly I saw a dog coming out from beside his slain master on the battlefield. He rushed forward toward us and then returned to his retreat uttering mournful cries. He licked the face of his master and darted toward us again; it seemed as if he was seeking aid and vengeance at the same time. Whether it was my state of mind, or the place, the time, the weather, the act itself, or I know not what, never has anything, on all my fields of battle, made such an impression upon me. I stopped involuntarily to contemplate the spectacle; that man, I said to myself, perhaps has friends, perhaps he has them in the camp, in his company, and yet he lies here abandoned by all except his dog.

What is man! and what the mystery of his impressions! I had ordered battles without emotion, battles which were to decide the fate of the army; I had seen, dry-eyed, movements executed which brought about the loss of a great number of our soldiers; here I was moved to tears. What is certain is that at the moment I must have been more favorably disposed toward a suppliant enemy. I better understood Achilles surrendering Hector's body to Priam's tears.

Napoleon Bonaparte

As Much As They

A dear and wise and exquisite child drew a plan for a headstone on the grave of a favorite terrier. She wrote the memorial verse for the headstone, including the words »*Who* died« on such and such a day, but the older and more worldly sculptor who cut the words into the stone changed them, since the memorial was to the little dog, to read »*Which* died« on such and such a day. The little girl saw the change and said to me with displeasure, »Wasn't my dog a *who* as much as the others laid to rest here?« And wasn't she right?

John Brown

Picking Flowers

I must tell you a feat of my dog Beau. Walking by the river side, I observed some water-lilies floating at a little distance from the bank. They are a large white flower, with an orange-colored eye, very beautiful. I had a desire to gather one, and, having your long cane in my hand, by the help of it endeavored to bring one of them within my reach. But the attempt proved vain, and I walked forward.

Beau had all the while observed me attentively. Returning soon after toward the same place, I observed him plunge into the river, while I was about forty yards distance from him; and, when I had nearly reached the spot, he swam to land with a lily in his mouth, which he came and laid at my foot.

William Cowper

Canine Fidelity

In September, 1929, blind Joseph Mellillo received his Bachelor of Arts degree from the University of Newark and a prize for the highest scholastic average over four years. The following day his seeing-eye dog Bonzo was publicly presented with this citation by the President of the University:

Faithful friend, devoted attendant, patient guide regularly present at all classes throughout the complete college course, partner in your master's *magna cum laude,* the University of Newark honors you for those qualities which have made you a familiar and inspiring figure in its halls. You have spoken seldom, but when your voice has been raised it always commanded attention, and at times your audible yawns have been the perfect echo of the unspoken reflections of your fellow-students. As President of the University, it is my distinguished privilege to confer upon you the honorary degree of *Canine Fidelity.*

Sharing With a Friend

Thirty years ago I was living in St. George's Square, Pimlico, and near me resided a well-known journalist, Mr. Percy Gregg. He had a little black and tan dog, Jimmie, for which I found a home when his master was about to leave London. It was reported to me that Jimmie always left my house after breakfast. At first some alarm was felt that he would stray; but as he invariably returned after an hour's stroll, I felt no anxiety.

But I learned that whenever he went away, he carried off a bone or something edible with him. I watched him one or two mornings squeeze through the area railings, on each occasion carrying a big bone, which he had great difficulty in steering through the iron bars. Being curious about the destination of the food, I followed him.

I tracked him to an empty house, next to that in which his former owner had lived. In the cellar in the area there lived a half-starved, ownerless terrier, who, I suppose, had once been a friend of Jimmie's, and whom my dog, in his days of prosperity, never forgot. Regularly the good little fellow trotted off to the empty cellar, and divided his morning's meal with his poor friend.

Thomas Hamler

What My Dog Means To Me

In 1947, when John Morrison of Rochester, New York, was eight years old, he won a prize offered by a local club for this essay:

My dog means somebody nice and quiet to be with. He does not say »Do!« like my mother, or »Don't!« like my father, or »Stop!« like my brother. My dog, Spot, and I sit together quietly and I like him and he likes me. The end.

A Slippery Rescue

One of the »rescues« made by a Seeing Eye dog had its humor as well as its thrills. In winter in northern Minnesota streets are frequently covered, for weeks at a time, with ice several inches deep. When they are not properly sanded they may be exceedingly slippery and dangerous. A young woman and her dog were crossing such a street, picking their way warily, when the dog noted an automobile turn out of a filling-station and come toward them. The dog stepped up its pace slightly to avoid the car but its mistress slipped and fell.

She was directly in the path of the automobile. Stopping was impossible. The ice was as slippery as greased glass. What the dog thought of the situation is impossible to know. What he did was important. Without a second's hesitation, it put its shoulders into the harness and dragged its mistress across the ice-sheeted street to the opposite curb. Depositing her, safe but still seated, in the gutter, the dog turned and licked her face as if to say, »Whew, that was a close one.«

Dickson Hartwell

Traveling With Charley

Charley likes to get up early, and he likes me to get up early too. And why shouldn't he? Right after his breakfast he goes back to sleep. Over the years he has developed a number of innocent-appearing ways to get me up. He can shake himself and his collar loud enough to wake the dead. If that doesn't work he gets a sneezing fit. But perhaps his most irritating method is to sit quietly beside the bed and stare into my face with a sweet and forgiving look on his face; I come out of deep sleep with the feeling of being looked at. But I have learned to keep my eyes tight shut. If I even blink he sneezes and stretches, and that night's sleep is over for me. Often the war of wills goes on for quite a time, I squinching my eyes shut and he forgiving me, but he nearly always wins. He liked traveling so much he wanted to get started early, and early for Charley is the first tempering of darkness with the dawn.

John Steinbeck

Epitaph On A Dog's Grave In Maryland

Major
Born a dog
Died a gentleman

Anonymous

An American War Dog

Chips' outfit landed just east of Licata at a spot on Sicily's southern coast known as Blue Beach. It was near this area where the crucial point of the entire operation developed when the German Hermann Goering and Fifteenth Armored divisions launched a tank-supported attack driving the Americans, at one point, back to the sea.

And it was here that Chips became the first American dog hero of the Second World War.

Chips was led ashore by Private John R. Rowell, who had returned to duty after being discharged from the Casablanca hospital.

Rowell and Chips cautiously advanced in the early morning blackness and were at a point about three hundred yards inland from the water when red-hot lead suddenly and unexpectedly began pouring at them from the darkness ahead, spraying the beach area. The firing came from two machine guns in a pill-box, which had been completely camouflaged as a peasant's hut.

Yankee soldiers threw themselves flat, hugging the sand.

Here Chips demonstrated the reckless insubordination that sometimes makes wartime heroes. Without waiting for an order from his handler to attack, Chips broke loose and, with teeth bared, charged the machinegun nest, completely disregarding the steady deadly stream of bullets.

Private Rowell describes what happened then as follows:

»There was an awful lot of noise and the firing stopped. Then I saw one Italian soldier come out the door with Chips at his throat. I called him off before he could kill the man.« Three others followed holding their hands above their heads.

In a few brief and dangerous seconds, this American war dog singlehanded and at great risk of his own life eliminated an enemy machinegun position and saved the lives of many of his comrades. His bravery enabled the inland advance to continue.

Clayton Going

Watch-Dog

'Tis sweet to hear the watch-dog's honest bark
Bay deep-mouth'd welcome as we draw near home;
'Tis sweet to know there is an eye will mark
Our coming, and look brighter when we come.

George Gordon, Lord Byron

Huskies

And never were dogs or men more faithful than
those poor brutes.
Day after day they struggled back across that
awful frozen desert,
Fighting for their lives and ours; day after
day they worked
Till the last ounce of strength was gone from them,
And then fell dead in their tracks without a sound,
Forty-one of them out of the forty-two with which
I left the »lost cache.«

Cmdr. Robert E. Peary

If you pick up a starving dog and make him prosperous, he will not bite you. That is the principal difference between a dog and a man.

Mark Twain

A High-Mannered Gentleman

To follow for ten minutes in the street some swaggering canine cavalier is to receive a lesson in dramatic art and the cultured conduct of the body. In every act and gesture you see him true to a refined conception. For a high-mannered and high-minded gentleman, careless, affable and gay, is the inborn pretension of the dog.

Robert Louis Stevenson

All the Good Dogs

What purpose did they serve, all the good dogs that once ran through the world and wait now in the shadowy quiet of the past?

They lightened our burdens and drove away our enemies and stayed when others left us. They gave aid and comfort, protection and security. They held a mirror wherein we might see ourselves as we long to be. They gave us a glimpse of the world beyond the narrow confines of our own species.

Although we make dull students, slowly they help us learn how to command and to protect with wisdom and justice and imagination.

They taught and still teach us the joy of giving generosity and kindness and love—without thought of gainful return.

And now—all the fleet hounds, the staunch mastiffs, the loyal shepherds, the dancing toys, the fumbling puppies, pets on silk pillows, workers plodding at their tasks, the special ones you loved best, those of ours we still miss—all the good dogs, goodbye, until on some brighter day, in some fairer place you run out again to greet us.

George and Helen Papashvily

Set at The Castle Press in Trump Mediäval,
a Venetian face designed by Professor
Georg Trump, in Munich. Printed on
Hallmark Eggshell Book paper.
Designed by Harald Peter.